The Bizarre Existence of a Detergent-Eating Anime Queen

Adam Manning

BookLeaf
Publishing

Presentation by *BookLeaf Publishing*

Web: www.bookleafpub.com

E-mail: info@bookleafpub.com

ISBN: 9789357613965

First edition 2022

This is dedicated to Dad,

Who never saw me achieve anything before he died, so now I'll finally achieve something in his name instead.

ACKNOWLEDGEMENT

First off, biggest thanks to Emma for finally help me realise what I want to do in life - write. More thanks goes to her for being a writing partner for well over a decade now on various things from Harry Potter roleplay to crafting our own private universe.

Also, I guess I should give thanks to the Open University for their recommended textbooks; I may not be smart enough to do a degree or masters myself (I'll leave that to Emma), but I am smart enough to read textbooks that are basically course materials, and they have really helped me get the mechanics of writing down.

And finally, I'd like to thank Mum, who does nothing but worry about me, and I love her for it, but hopefully this book can serve as the start of some evidence to ease that worry, that I'll be alright, that I've got this.

PREFACE

I've never been hugely keen on poetry, however, there has always been one form that I really enjoy - haiku. It is all thanks to when I first played one particular level on "Spyro 3: Year Of The Dragon", a platform adventure game for the original PlayStation as a child.

"Spooky Swamp" was a level in which you had to navigate a dark, rainy swamp finding giant tealights in little treetop cabins and having to light them with Spyro's flame breath. The inhabitants of this swamp all spoke weird and confused me somewhat as a child until I reached a recurring character in the game called Moneybags. He was now speaking weirdly too and while I never liked him, his new way of speaking intrigued me. I paid him some of my hard-earned gems (grumble grumble) and he said,

"Best of all, Spyro...
I can now stop speaking Haiku.
What a sweet relief!"

My ten year old brain suddenly remembered that word - haiku. We had learned about them at school once and it had always stuck with me as "that 5 7 5 thing". I then ran all the way back to the beginning of the level and talked to all the inhabitants of the swamp again, counting the syllables. 5-7-5, over and over again. Every time I played that one level again after that discovery, I would make up little random Spyro-related haiku in my head for the next hour or two.

This is just a long-winded way of saying that a good chunk of these poems are haiku, but as is the strange mix that is my life, there are some non-haiku poems as well, some forms I've never tried before too. It was really fun to look back and reminisce while writing these, despite some tears halting the writing process for one or two of them.

I hope you enjoy these poems as much as I enjoyed replaying Spyro 3 just to get that Moneybags quote.

Here We Go

Day one of my first
WriteAngle poem challenge.
I might do haiku.

Japan Makes Other Things Too

Swimming pools, skull kicks,
Magical girls slam popstars.
Joshi wrestling rules.

Suplexing Lewis

3

That wrestling advice,
We never used to listen.
"Don't try this at home."

Do Try This Home

They always ask, "what's so great about
VRChat?"
You can escape from jail or swim in champagne,
You can experience it all from wherever you're
sat.

Becoming best friends with strangers just like
that,
For an hour or two and never again,
They always ask, "what's so great about
VRChat?"

Roaming the streets of Paris dressed like a cat,
Not having to worry about catching a plane,
You can experience it all from wherever you're
sat.

Ears filled with voices of all people that
Are trying their best to be heard on a train,
I sometimes ask "what's so great about
VRChat?"

There's even full weddings held in this format,
So invite the Americans, those from Germany,
Spain,

You can experience it all from wherever you are
sat.

Of course, like the real world, you'll find the odd
twat,
But overall the joys far exceed any pain,
So when they ask "what's so great about
VRChat?"
I say you can experience it from wherever you
are sat.

Back To Basics

6

My first villanelle,
It went pretty well I think.
But I like haiku.

twitch.com/leosault

Playing games online
Or watching friends mess around.
I talk to Chat fondly.

The VRChat Singer

8

I once found on Twitch
A man singing Disney songs.
He was in VR??

TFMJonny

It all began in 2019
While browsing around on Twitch,
An anime boy showed up on my screen
Singing in perfect pitch.

I thought to myself, "Woah! This is obscene!"
He sung Disney songs unlike any other,
"His voice hits every note so clean!"
After nailing one song he would then smash
another!

But after singing some songs, he would just chat
in between
To friends or strangers alike,
He'd adjust his VR cam to make sure they're on
screen
And speak into his handheld mic.

After a few months of watching I joined the VR
scene
To meet online friends from chat,
We all hung out on Jonny's singing stream
My avatar was part-cat.

And so now we shift to the Tide Pod Queen

The birth of my online "brand",
It started as an improv scene
That's gone completely out of hand.

You see, Jonny used to switch to a screen
That played a video of his making.
To "Tide Pod Lolis", this vid was mean
And it left my heart aching.

So I vowed to help and became their Queen
With Jonny as our foe,
I'd protest on stream and anywhere in between,
Until he addressed my woe.

A year or so had passed and our roleplay war
had been
Harmless but always fun,
But with COVID springing up unforeseen
Obsession with online chats begun.

People used apps like Skype to see Nan on a
screen,
More people also joined VR,
But Jonny took advantage of both in quarantine
And his talent would take him far.

Using an online chat site, "Omegle" (which isn't
always clean...)
He sung for strangers live,

He recorded the performance and reactions,
mostly keen
And uploaded to YouTube where he began to
thrive.

His videos got thrusted into the YouTube
machine
Shown to everyone during their darkest days,
That strange singing wolf boy lit up people's
quarantine
And he became an online craze.

Three years later and what a three years it's been
He earned that gold play button,
The award for a million subscribers that gleams
In a basement in Edmonton.

Lightsource Gaming

12

Minecraft adventures,
Exploring weird Far Cry maps.
Not great YouTubers.

My First Game

13

It was my ninth year
A game was given to me.
Bugs Bunny, fun times.

Fantasy Football

14

Did he score today?
Let's check his fantasy points.
Red card, minus-two.

He's Football Crazy, Football Mad

7am on a Sunday morning
"Keep it down" was my only warning
Match Of The Day on the TV
I'd set up the front room ready to be
My football pitch for the next two hours
To emulate the show from BBC Towers

Shearer, Cole, Yorke and Scholes
I'd run around the room and copy their goals
The fire guard was a perfect replica of the net
The other goal, just gaps between chairs, the
best I could get
I'd mumble my own commentary to myself
And cheer victories alone using darts trophies
from Dad's shelf

A small sponge ball is what I would use
And used so much the filling would ooze
Out of a tear from its faux-leather shell
A clear sign that I used this ball well
I'd poke the stuffing back in time and again
And go back to practice a top corner pen

Only once did anything get smashed

The glass shade of an oil lamp unfortunately crashed
To the floor, and I got into big trouble
I'd only been pretending the Toon won the Double
But soon my living room football pitch came to an end
When Dad made two goals in a field to defend

I used to spend hours in that small little field
That once lit up my face when Dad had revealed
That he had found old nets he could attach
To the wooden goals and I could emulate Match
Of The Day once again and just like before
Spend all of my time making up the score.

Dad (sad version)

Breakfast at seven, dinner at one
Tea and relaxing from six until nine
Dad never had much time for fun
Working the farm took up most of his time

Except Friday nights he'd go out for darts
He kept to this schedule just like a clock
But Mum and Dad's marriage eventually parts
So moving out was a bit of a shock

Only seeing him once a week was strange
But in a weird way I was used to it
Only coming in for meals without change
I'd grown to only seeing him for a bit

In later years he'd go on more days out
With the step kids and myself to all kinds of
locations
To him at the time I was an unemployed lout
But I had no idea what I wanted when it came to
vocations

But then the news came, he only had a few
months left
And my brain just decided to shut everything out

Fate performing the ultimate theft
Before I could prove I was no lout

Don't get me wrong, I do love my Dad
He did so much for me overall
But out of all the time together we had
I wish those times weren't so small

I wish I made more of an effort to know you,
Dad
Instead of the brief times we could only talk
small
Thank you for raising me as well as you could in
the time you had
And now I've found what I can do, I promise I
will give it my all.

Dad (happy version)

Always willing to play darts if asked
Playing any kind of sport was a blast
Especially football which you did not care for
But still tested my keeper skills which I'm sure
was a chore
You played the best, Dad.

You made bases for us out of all kinds of stuff
Trees, silage wrap, bales, didn't matter, they
were never rough
Bale fortresses thirty feet high were the best
Even if our BB gun warfare had you stressed
You built the best, Dad.

You taught me how to drive a tractor
Despite my lack of interest in farming being a
factor
You taught me basic woodwork too
Something I never would have found interesting
if it wasn't you
You taught the best, Dad.

You found the secret passage way on my Harry
Potter game

And completing a Crash Bandicoot level you
can claim
But you were terrible at FIFA, you just could not
get a hold
And when I asked about Prince Of Persia, you
said you were too old!
You tried the best, Dad.

Making everyone laugh, that's what I remember
most
Amongst friends, amongst family, with the guy
delivering fenceposts
Making people smile at the Milky Way darts
With actual humour and not relying on dad jokes
or farts
You amused the best, Dad.

Everyone's friend, everyone's rock
The king of maintaining tons of livestock
The father who sweat and toiled for us
Even when we made way too much fuss
You ARE the best, Dad.

Darts Friday?

21

Playing at the pub
We had special shirts we wore.
We finished bottom.

Going Town Tonight?

Music is too loud,
All girls are drunk or taken.
How do we converse?

A Limerick for Aria

There is one who happens to be
All the parts that are missing from me
She's smart and for this
I will not get a kiss
All I'll get is a big and loud "REEEEEE"

Butlins

24

With her and her fam
We went to see the wrasslin',
Oi! Sit down in front!
It's okay though, we mostly
Went for the food and arcades.

The Rarest Superheroes In The Universe

As a matter of fact I just happen to be
One in fifteen thousand with this special malady
Phenylketonuria to be very precise
It's a metabolic condition which can be quite
nice
There is a lot of camaraderie between us
afflicted
We have forged friendships we never would've
predicted

We must maintain a low protein diet
No meat, eggs or fish, don't even try it
But that pesky enzyme that we can't process
Is also in bread, flour and some drinks, which is
a bit of a mess
There are companies that specialise in
replacement food
And supplements we need that have to be
brewed

These companies gather once a year
At a conference held by the charity that we're
All invited to as PKU-havers, it's great

As a child you're amazed at how much can be
ate
Whole tables of new low protein products to try
And a hotel staff taught what can or can't fly

One of the best things about these kind of deals
Is the new ideas and tasting of low protein meals
That parents never realised that they could make
Using bread, pasta, and flour that's all fake
You may think gluten & lactose free food tastes
the worst
But we were the guinea pigs who tried it all first

Bread rolls like polystyrene, cheese like rubber
Us PKU 90s kids were always the snubber
Of this replacement "food" until they finally got
it right
The fake chocolate bars were always an absolute
delight
But there was always one issue for all of us
Our supplements were always everyone's biggest
fuss

We all had our different go-to drinks
But no matter which you had, everyone thinks
That they all taste horrid and are almost
undrinkable
But to go with out them was completely
unthinkable

So most of us grin and bared the vile grog
Whether it be Vitaflo, Maxamum or Analog

But this experience we shared of food and
hardships
Brought us closer together and we made
friendships
That will last for a lifetime from meeting when
young
And every year we go back, the friendship has
clung
To our memories of that very first time we
Met and realised there were "others like me".

The Boys

One fateful day on the bus to town
I met an old friend who shared my frown
We both had just dealt with the DWP
And their bullshit reasons not to give us our
money
We got chatting about the one night that
He yelled with cramp at 3am, the night I met
Matt
We spent the whole journey chatting about
Wrestling and gaming and a friendship did
sprout
We exchanged gamertags and then
Later that night became Xbox friends
We played all kinds of things but mostly GTA
Online
I'd not really done multiplayer before but it was
fine
And through Matt I met his gaming crew
Will, Ed, Gavin and Scott too
We all became as thick as thieves
So much that when anyone leaves
The party in which we all yap
Would playfully joke that they were crap
Myself and Gavin were particularly bad
At racing in GTA but we never got mad

We even ran around the entire map on foot
And had funny moments me and Gavin put
On YouTube to tens of views
But it didn't matter because we were the best of
crews
And while these days we may be more apart
We'll never get tired of hearing Matt fart.

The End

It's been a strange thing,
My life in haiku and rhymes.
Thank you for reading.